Usborne

Write Your Own

Mystery and Ghost Stories

Usborne

Write Your Own

Mystery and Ghost Stories

With stories by...

Write your name here.

Contents

Story writing section

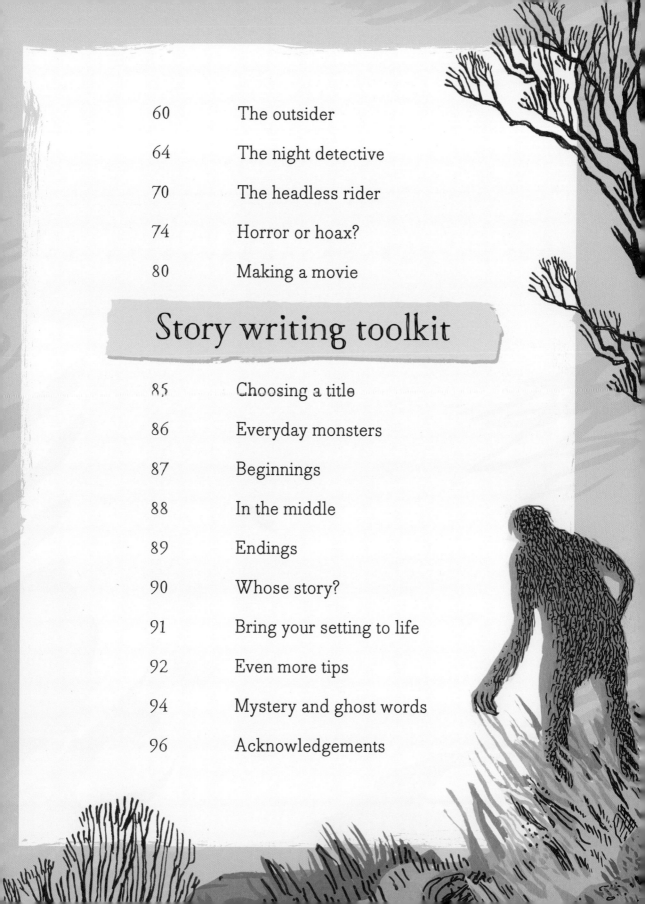

Story writing toolkit

What's a mystery story?

A mystery story usually begins with a problem or puzzle that needs to be solved, and a main character who sets about solving it. There are lots of different types of mystery story.

Natural or supernatural?

Some mystery stories are set firmly in the real world, and have a logical solution. Other mysteries are supernatural – perhaps a restless ghost is the source of the trouble?

Unsolved crimes

Many mystery stories are about a crime, and the process of solving it. The main character might be a professional detective or someone who solves crimes as a hobby.

Gone!

A missing person is often the 'puzzle' to solve in a mystery. Is it a kidnapping? Has the person run away? Or are stranger forces at work – perhaps there's an ancient mirror that sucks people in through their reflections?

Aunt in the attic

Family secrets can provide great starting points for mystery stories – from imprisoned relatives, secret twins and mistaken identities to stolen fortunes and family curses.

Open window **Snatched** DARK CORRIDOR HIDDEN DOOR
LOUD THUMP *Fluttering curtain* **Confession** Creepy

Here's what you'll need to write your own mystery story:

A puzzle

A secret, an unsolved crime, an unexplained event,
or something – or someone – that has gone missing.

An investigator

A character who tries to solve the mystery. This could be a person caught up
in events, or someone who hears about the mystery and sets out to solve it.

A threat

This could be a criminal, a ghost, or another menacing presence
lurking at the heart of the story.

Clues

Hints that help the reader guess at what might be the solution to
the mystery. Sometimes, the reader might even solve the mystery
before the main character does.

Misdirection

Red herrings, or false clues, that lead the reader in the wrong
direction and make the mystery harder to solve.

Suspense and tension

Create uncertainty about what might happen next, and a fear
that it will be something bad. Will the puzzle be solved?
What will happen if it isn't?

A solution?

By the end of a mystery story, the puzzle is usually
solved – although some stories leave lingering
questions and doubts in the reader's mind.

Missing glove **Strange whispers** Unexplained Murky
Disappearance Rooted to the spot SNOOPING *Howling winds*

Planning your story

Your readers should be able to follow the story, or plot, as it unfolds, but they shouldn't be able to predict the outcome. By planning your story, you can decide what information to give away – and when.

Beginning

1) Introduce your main character. Create a sense of unease by dropping hints and clues that something is wrong.

A nurse notices that a picture keeps falling off a wall in the old hospital.

2) Transform the sense of unease into a problem the character can't ignore.

The nurse sees a ghostly face appear in a mirror before it cracks.

Keep your readers gripped by ending each stage of your story with a cliffhanger.

Middle

3) Your character investigates the problem. Build the tension with surprising revelations.

The nurse finds old newspapers revealing that the hospital hauntings often occur at times of trouble.

4) How does the story reach its climax (its most exciting point)?

A clue from the newspapers leads the nurse into the dark hospital basement, where she confronts the ghost.

Bring your story climax to life by setting it in a dramatic location.

End

5) Your main character pieces together the evidence to solve the problem.

The ghost is friendly! It's been trying to warn the nurse that an earthquake is coming. She evacuates the hospital and the hauntings stop.

You could surprise your readers with a plot twist at the end.

Your turn

Write a plan for a mystery story in the space below, using the one on the left to help you. You could end the first two stages with cliffhangers, and add a twist at the end.

Title *ne w n n rm e y i t o i*

Beginning *u r m n y t o i t n e r x o r n*

Middle

End

Here are two ideas to start you off:

You could write a story about a lonely child who discovers the school library is haunted...

...or about a singer who disappears suddenly after a show, then sends a letter to a friend asking for help.

Planting clues

As well as outlining the key events of your story, plan when you will drop clues for your reader.

Try to include a clue or two in each section, with a final clue near the end that helps your character solve the mystery.

Creating characters

Before you start writing a story, you'll need to create a main character – a 'protagonist' – and an 'antagonist', a character who gets in the way of what the protagonist wants.

Fill in the profiles below, and start thinking how you can bring your characters to life.

Protagonist

This could be someone who's investigating a haunting, or who has witnessed some kind of terrible crime.

Weak points

Give your protagonist weaknesses as well as strengths. It helps build tension in the story if there's a chance the protagonist might not succeed.

Name

Does he/she have any special abilities?

What are his/her distinguishing features?

Does he/she have a sidekick or any close friends?

What is his/her greatest ambition?

What is he/she afraid of?

What words best describe him/her?

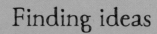

Finding ideas

Feeling stuck? You could borrow a character from a book or a film, and add new traits to make it your own. Alternatively, take someone you've read about in a newspaper or magazine. You could even star in your story, along with your friends.

Antagonist

This might be a kidnapper, or a ghost that becomes dangerous when it's disturbed.

More than skin deep

Give your characters personal struggles that your reader can identify with, such as a deep regret or a fear of loneliness. Once your reader begins to care about your characters, there's more at stake when things start to go wrong...

Name

What does he/she/it look like?

What drives him/her/it?

Does he/she/it have any strange habits?

Does anything make him/her/it happy?

How does the antagonist react when he/she/it is angry?

What frightens him/her/it?

Building suspense

Suspense is the feeling of nervous excitement you experience when you're kept guessing about what's going to happen next. It's especially important in mystery and ghost stories.

Long and short

One way to build suspense is to vary the length of your sentences. Long sentences slow down the pace and create a feeling that time is dragging, forcing your reader to wait to find out what happens next.

> The masked girl lowered herself down from the ceiling, tensing every muscle as she hovered over the Ancient Greek vase.

Short sentences speed up the pace and stop your story feeling too monotonous. They're useful for high-energy action scenes.

> She flinched.
> An infrared sensor!

Continue writing the scene below about a mysterious girl trying to snatch a vase from a museum. Try to vary the length of your sentences.

A single bead of sweat fell from the tip of her nose to the floor below, as she hung from the wire, staring intently at the vase.

12

Tick, tick, tick...

Another way to build suspense is to give your characters a limited time to achieve their goals. As your characters race against the clock, the reader will feel a sense of urgency and panic.

Continue the story of the masked girl below. Add references to time ticking to keep the tension high.

The masked girl checked her watch as it counted down: 1:59, 1:58, 1:57... She had less than two minutes to escape before the entire building was in lockdown.

Dropping hints

In longer stories, avoid revealing everything to your reader at once. Drop hints that something intriguing is going to happen, but don't reveal *what* until later on.

The masked girl leapt across the roof, but she couldn't shake the feeling that someone was following her...

Suspense happens in between the moments of action – it's the promise that something exciting will happen soon.

Talk the talk

When characters talk to each other, it's called 'dialogue'.
Dialogue helps to bring characters to life, and can also
be an exciting way to move the action along.

Different voices

Some people chatter. Others speak slowly. Some people hardly
use any words at all. Create distinctive characters by including
lots of different voices in your stories. Here's an example:

"Lady Montgomery." Inspector Roberts coughed.
"I have been told that a leopard's gone walkies
from London Zoo. Goes by the name of Spots.
Ring any bells, does it, ma'am?"

"Heavens above! What on earth are you
suggesting, young man?" Lady Montgomery replied.
"I wish to speak to my lawyer immediately."

Continue the dialogue below.

Add action

To keep your story gripping, try breaking up dialogue with action that moves the plot forward. For example, a criminal might do something that hints at his or her guilt.

Roberts paused to take a sip of his coffee. "Now ma'am. I ain't got time to beat around the bush. Tell me - wheredja get that lovely fur coat you're wearin'?"

Lady Montgomery shifted in her seat. "It's an old family heirloom, my dear."

Continue the dialogue below, including both dialogue and action.

Speech tags

Phrases such as 'he said'/'she said' are known as 'speech tags'. They act as signposts to show the reader *who* is saying *what*. Stick to simple speech tags – if you vary them too much, you'll distract your reader. For example:

"Time's up," Roberts said.

"What do you mean?" Lady Montgomery replied.

"I'm takin' you down to the cell ma'am," Roberts said.

...sounds better than:

"Time's up," Roberts growled.

"What do you mean?" Lady Montgomery whimpered.

"I'm taking you down to the cell, ma'am," Roberts exclaimed.

Story writing section

Your stories

The following pages are packed with ideas and suggestions to help you write your own mystery and ghost stories. There's a 'Story writing toolkit' on pages 84-95 with more writing tips and suggestions.

Write your story titles here
(after you've written them).

18
24
28
34
40
44
50
54
60
64
70
74
80

The haunted house

You're lost in a forest, and it's growing dark. Through the trees you spot a house that seems to be empty. It doesn't look very welcoming – the windows are shattered and some are boarded up. But you've got no choice – you need somewhere to shelter for the night.

Write your story title here.

Write a story about what happens during your night in the house. Use all five senses to describe the atmosphere.

What can you SEE through the window? Is that a face in the glass, or a trick of the light?

Can you HEAR doors slamming upstairs? Or is it just the wind?

Does the air FEEL cold and clammy?

Where is that old, musty SMELL coming from?

What is that unpleasant TASTE in the back of your throat?

What is inside the house? Is it something supernatural? Perhaps it's a family of ghosts, or a lonely spirit looking for fun?

Is whatever's inside the house welcoming you in or trying to get you to leave? How is it making its presence known to you?

Continued...

Goosebumps

SPINE-TINGLING

Footsteps

Apparition

Wailing

SICKENING

Bone-chilling

SHUDDER

Rustling

SCRATCHING

Rocking

Chased

Shatter

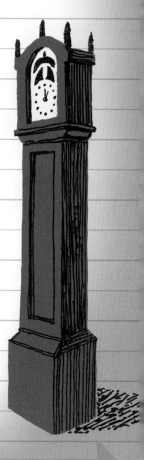

Continued...

As you explore the house, build tension by creating false alarms that surprise your reader.

I heard noises behind the door, so I flung it open... It was just a cat!

I felt something tickling my neck and spun around. A cobweb!

The relief that comes after the false alarm will lull your reader into a false sense of security, so that when the truly scary things take place, they are even more shocking.

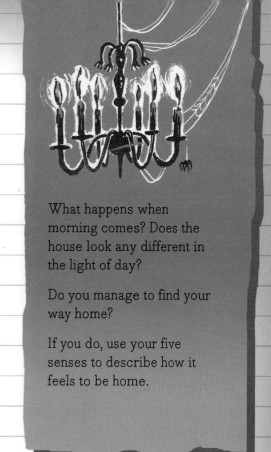

What happens when morning comes? Does the house look any different in the light of day?

Do you manage to find your way home?

If you do, use your five senses to describe how it feels to be home.

A poltergeist journal

A poltergeist (meaning 'noisy ghost' in German) is a type of ghost that is said to cause physical disturbances – it may throw furniture around or pinch people who get in its way.

Write your story title here.

Imagine your character is being haunted by a poltergeist. Write a story in the form of a journal about his or her experience.

What tricks does the poltergeist play?

How do your character's friends, parents and teachers react?

Poltergeist habits

Poltergeists are said to attach themselves to people, especially teenagers, and take energy from them.

They are invisible, and can cause objects to shake or fly across a room.

Monday

Describing emotions

When people are feeling stressed, frightened or anxious, they often experience physical changes in their bodies.

What changes does your character experience while under attack from the poltergeist?

Try some of these sorts of descriptions in your writing:

MY HANDS FELT CLAMMY.

The hair on my arms stood upright.

MY TONGUE FELT LIKE SANDPAPER.

A sheen of sweat gathered on my forehead.

Continued...

Thursday

Friday

Apports

Objects that are moved by poltergeists are known as *apports*. Sometimes, apports can appear as if from nowhere.

Describe what sort of apports your character sees. School books? Old socks? Oranges and lemons?

Saturday

Sunday

DRAGGED OUT OF BED

Floating through the air

FLAMES FROM NOWHERE

Moody

STRESSED

Best friend

BABBLING VOICES

Nervous

ECHOING YELLS

Banging and thumping

ANGRY TEACHER

Late for class

HURLED ACROSS THE ROOM

Homework

DETENTION

SMASHED PLATES

Lights flickered

Kidnapped!

A bell rings through the empty corridors of an expensive boarding school in the country. Then all is quiet.
Soon, whispers begin about the maths teacher, Miss Mildert. She's been been kidnapped! Who did it? Why?

Write a story about a student who decides to investigate the mystery. The opening line has been written for you.

Write your story title here.

Story ideas

Who is hiding secrets, and who carried out the abduction?

How was Miss Mildert kidnapped? Is she being held to ransom? (That's when someone demands money to return a victim.)

Where does your student begin hunting for clues? Has anything suspicious been left behind?

Can your student character solve the mystery before the police?

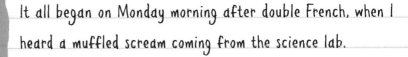

It all began on Monday morning after double French, when I heard a muffled scream coming from the science lab.

Trennyex ♡ xx o xox

A trail of clues

Try connecting your clues together. Finding one clue might lead to another, and help the student – and the reader – solve the mystery of the missing maths teacher.

Here's an example:

Clue 1: In the science lab, I found a note on the desk which read, 'Meet in the dining hall at 8pm.'

Clue 2: On the floor of the dining hall, Miss Mildert's wool jacket lay in a crumpled heap...

Clue 3: The usually timid dinner lady had a bandage wrapped around her fist...

Continued...

Red herrings

Are there any red herrings, or false clues, that distract the student and lead him or her down the wrong path?

Red herrings help to set back an investigation, and make life harder for the main character. They make the mystery more challenging and exciting to read, before it's finally solved.

For example, your character could:

- Misunderstand a snippet of conversation at lunch.

- Discover a misleading note in a teacher's diary.

- Find a stain on a desk that looks like blood. It turns out to be tomato sauce.

Add your own below:

Suspects and motives

Keep your reader guessing by including a number of suspects (people who *may* be guilty of the crime) who all have different motives (reasons for doing it).

Here are some examples:

Suspect: Head girl

Motive: Failed her maths exam and needs to fake her results so she can get into university.

Suspect: The mother of a student who didn't get into the school.

Motive: Seeking revenge for refusing to help her child cheat on the school's entry exams.

Fingerprints

HUNTING FOR EVIDENCE

Continued...

Evidence and alibis

Can your student uncover any evidence (information that proves someone is guilty)? Perhaps there's a lipstick print on a glass, or a broken pair of glasses on the floor...

And do any of your suspects have an alibi (proof that he or she was somewhere else at the time of the crime)? Perhaps the head girl was playing a lacrosse match on the day of the kidnapping?

A solution?

Is the kidnapper caught in the end? How? Does Miss Mildert return safe and sound?

Or does the mystery remain unsolved? Perhaps the student finds out the truth but no one will believe the young investigator.

Maybe Miss Mildert is never seen again – but a huge ransom is paid into a mysterious bank account, then someone who looks *very similar* to her is seen on an expensive yacht a few years later...

IT ROOM   Ransom note   **Locked door**   Blackboard

Mystery phone call   SCHOOL BULLY   Secret study room

Haunted painting

A boy is rooting through some old junk in his grandmother's attic, when he discovers a painting covered in dust. He brings it downstairs, and soon realizes that something is not quite right... it's haunted.

Write your story title here.

The haunted painting is shown here on the right. Write a story about what happens next.

Questions

Who is the girl in the painting?

Does the boy recognize anything? The girl? The doll? Or the room itself?

Whose shadow is lurking in the background?

What's written in the letter on the desk?

An element of doubt

Build the tension in your story by throwing in an element of doubt.

Perhaps the boy catches something moving out of the corner of his eye. Was it the painting, or was it just his active imagination?

Your reader will feel a sense of anticipation as he or she waits to find out what happens.

Continued...

More than meets the eye...

Often, ghosts have unfinished business they want to resolve. Think about what unfinished business might be connected to the painting.

- Is there a family secret, such as a terrible crime or a tragic death, that is about to be exposed?

- Is the girl in the painting seeking revenge for her own murder?

- Is she trying to warn the boy about something? Perhaps the boy's grandmother is not who she seems?

Continued...

EERIE

Hypnotic

DISTURBING

Possessed

GRIM

Nightmarish

CURSED

LOOMING SHADOW

Wicked

PIERCING GAZE

Deathly pale

SINISTER

Written in blood

ANCESTOR

ORPHANAGE

MOVING EYES

OUTSTRETCHED

Recoiled

EVIL

PRICKLING

A locked room mystery

A priceless sculpture has been stolen from a top floor apartment in a high-rise block. No one knows how the thief got in: the room was securely locked from the inside when the police arrived. Who can crack this case wide open?

Write a story about someone who tries to solve this seemingly-impossible riddle.

Is your investigator a police detective? Or an outsider they've called in – maybe he or she is a soldier who's trained to storm into secure locations? Or a former criminal who's an expert at breaking into buildings?

Was there only one thief, or was it a conspiracy (a plot involving several different people working together)?

How did the thief get away with it? Did someone climb in through the air vents? Are there any false walls?

Maybe the sculpture is still hidden in the apartment? Could the thief have hidden under a trapdoor and left after the police had gone? Perhaps the lock was digital and hacked from outside?

Write your story title here.

How-dunnit

Start by writing two timelines: one going over every detail of *how* the robbery was committed and another showing *how* the investigator works it out. That way you'll know what clues to drop and be ready to reveal all the answers at the end.

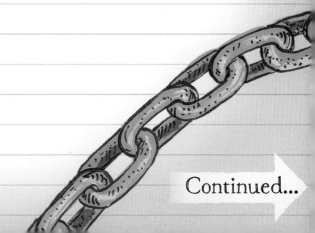

Continued...

Some ideas for clues that help the investigator solve the crime...

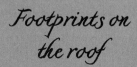

Footprints on the roof

Abseiling equipment found in the street below

A remote control handset

Secret passage behind a shower cubicle

A trapdoor concealed by a rug

WINDOW RECENTLY REPLACED

A trained monkey/ rodent/robot arm

SCRATCHES ON THE FLOOR WHERE FURNITURE HAS BEEN MOVED

MAGNET FOUND NEAR THE METAL DOOR LOCK

Crime scene reveal

In many mysteries, the investigator gathers all the suspects at the crime scene to explain who has done it and how. This has two advantages:

- It heightens the tension, as the suspects know the thief is among them.

- It brings the investigator's explanation to life. For example, if the sculpture is hidden in the apartment, the investigator could reaveal a false wall and SHOW it to the suspects, rather than just telling them what has happened.

Make sure your investigator's final explanation is logical – your reader should feel satisfied with the solution, not cheated.

Ghost train

A shadowy figure is on a station platform in the middle of nowhere. Through a cloud of fog, a train comes into view... but there's something unusual about it. Write a story about what happens when the person climbs onboard.

Write your story title here.

Some of the most unsettling stories describe something that *seems* familiar but is subtly different.

The feeling of fear and anxiety that follows is known as the 'uncanny'.

Think about how you would describe an ordinary train arriving into a station, and make it *slightly* different:

The train drew into the platform in silence.

There was nobody inside, not even a driver.

What is it like inside the train? Try replacing ordinary sights and sounds with unexpected ones.

Inside, the carriage was lined with mirrors.

Classical music blasted out at high volume over the intercom.

Where does the train stop next? Is it somewhere eerie and spooky?

She was about to step off the train, but looked down over the edge of a cliff.

Continued...

What happens on the journey?

Does the train drop its passengers off into a frightening other world? Perhaps it picks up unusual passengers along the way...

DEAD END

Empty siding

PLUMES OF SMOKE

GHOULISH CONDUCTOR

Rusty trucks

Spectral driver

WHISTLE

BLOOD-SPATTERED
BAGGAGE

Silent station

MISSING TRACKS

Stifled cries

DESERTED PLATFORM

Continued...

How does it end?

Does the train reach a final destination? Is the stranger who was waiting on the platform ever seen again?

Strange sleuths

A valuable diamond has been stolen from a famous museum. The police are baffled. The head of the museum turns to a brilliant private investigator with highly unusual methods...

Write your story title here.

Hidden strengths

Many mystery stories feature an eccentric, or unusual investigator.

What makes your investigator unusual? Does he or she have any strange hobbies? Or any other peculiar personality quirks?

These quirks could mask hidden strengths. For example, the unusual thought processes of a highly intelligent investigator might make him or her appear easily distracted to other people.

Perhaps your investigator is a daring child or a knitting-mad granny? If your character doesn't look like a typical detective, suspects might talk more freely in front of them.

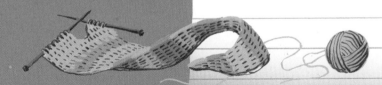

Sidekicks

Some investigators work with a friend or companion known as a sidekick.

A sidekick might have skills your investigator lacks. For example, if your investigator is socially awkward and uptight, your sidekick might be friendly and easy-going.

Sidekicks don't have to be human. What about a loyal dog who's an excellent judge of character?

Your sidekick can ask useful questions which help you explain your investigator's methods to the reader.

"How did you work out that the codes to the safe would be in her handbag?"

Continued...

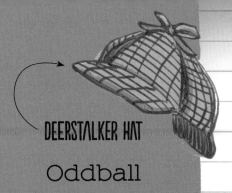

DEERSTALKER HAT

Oddball

Unassuming

QUIETLY LISTENING

Single-minded

DISGUISE

POWERS OF OBSERVATION

Restless

HAWK-EYED

Blundering

PHOTOGRAPHIC MEMORY

TWITCHY

Handlebar moustache

Intuition

Sixth sense

Cunning

PLUCKY SCHOOL CHILD

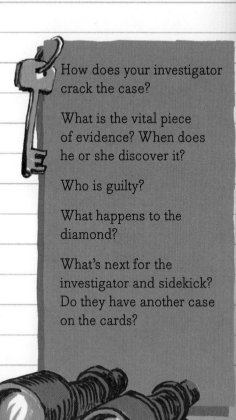

How does your investigator crack the case?

What is the vital piece of evidence? When does he or she discover it?

Who is guilty?

What happens to the diamond?

What's next for the investigator and sidekick? Do they have another case on the cards?

Ancient Egyptian curse

Archaeologists on a dig discover the tomb of an Ancient Egyptian pharaoh, which has lain undisturbed for thousands of years. Inside, there's a solid gold coffin engraved with hieroglyphics. The hieroglyphics read, "He who disturbs this coffin shall be cursed forever." What happens next?

Write your story title here.

Story ideas

What is it like inside the tomb? Stuffy? Dusty? Smelly? Chilly?

Is there any other treasure inside, apart from the golden coffin?

How do the archaeologists react to the hieroglyphics? Do they take them seriously? Or do they laugh?

Do they open the coffin? If so, what do they find? A mummy?

Does the curse take effect? If so, how? Do they all fall ill with a deadly disease? Do they lose all their money and possessions? Does the mummy come to life?

Know your history

You might find it helpful to look at some books about the Ancient Egyptians to find out more about them.

What are hieroglyphics? What is a mummy? How about a sarcophagus? What else might you find in an Egyptian tomb?

Continued...

Show not tell

Try to avoid *telling* your readers what to think. Instead, *show* them what's happening by describing a character's actions – it creates a more vivid experience. For example:

TELL:

The mummy was terrifying

SHOW:

The mummy rose up out of its coffin and slowly turned its bandaged head. Suddenly, its ragged mouth opened to let out a furious roar.

Continued...

SCARAB

Amulet

Deadly desert

TUTANKHAMUN

Pyramids

OBELISK

DECOMPOSED

The Nile

**THE VALLEY
OF THE KINGS**

TOMB RAIDERS

Eternal life

PAPYRUS

BLOODY
BANDAGES

FLESH-EATING BEETLE

Endings

Do the archaeologists manage to break the curse? If so, how? Do they return any ancient treasures back to where they belong? Maybe they just seal up the tomb, hoping that no one ever finds it again...

The outsider

Some friends are staying at a summer camp. One afternoon, a lonely figure dressed in rags wanders into the camp. Nobody knows who – or what – the figure is. Then, it begins to speak…

Write your story title here.

Imagine you are one of the friends at the camp when the stranger appears.

Write a story about what happens in the form of a letter home.

What did the stranger look like? Did it have long, ragged hair and a furry body? Or was it was covered in scales?

What did it say? Did it have a name? Where had it come from? What was it looking for? What did its voice sound like?

How did you react when the stranger spoke? Did you run away screaming? Or did you cautiously invite it over?

Dear...

Keep it real

Try to make your letter feel grounded in reality by giving detailed descriptions of your surroundings. If your story seems like something that could really happen, it will be scarier.

I felt a drop of rain on my shoulder, and shivered as a cold gust of wind swept across the camp.

The smell of beef stew, bubbling away on the camp fire, wafted under my nose.

When a story feels real, this is known as 'verisimilitude'.

Continued...

GNARLED

Hairy knuckles

Ghastly

Ragged stitches

GROTESQUE

Shrivelled

CLAWED HANDS

Lurking

Windswept

Weather-beaten

Yellowing teeth

Hunched over

Dragging feet

BLOODSHOT EYES

Monstrous

Hideous

FOUL STENCH

LIVING HELL

Miserable

Signing off

How do you finish your letter? Do you promise to write back with further news? Or do you sign off abruptly, leaving your reader guessing?

I must sign off now. It's late and I can hear something scratching outside – I don't have a clue what it could be... I'll write again soon.

Lots of love, John

The night detective

If a cursed object is found at the scene of a crime, or the number one suspect is a werewolf – who do you call? You need a specialist in the supernatural, a detective who knows how to banish evil spirits as well as follow clues...

Write your story title here.

Make up a detective who solves supernatural crimes and write a story about one of his or her cases.

As in any detective story, you need clues. But instead of fingerprints or footprints, your character could find a severed tentacle or a powerful spell scrawled on the wall.

What's the crime?
Who (or what) does your detective question?

Who is the criminal?
A supernatural creature?
A human with strange powers?

Does the detective use magic to solve the crime? A crystal ball? A spell that reveals who's been in a certain room in the last 24 hours?

Eerie origins

Knowing the background of your characters will help your reader understand what drives them.

Why would someone become a supernatural detective? Were your character's parents kidnapped by demons? Was she or he born with superpowers that made an ordinary life difficult? Or perhaps fighting the forces of darkness is the family business?

Continued...

Exorcism

Pentagram

Summoning

MYSTICAL

Ectoplasm

DEMON

GANGSTER

Distant
scream

Shocking
revelation

Trail of slime

Old enemies

A supernatural detective is likely to make some dangerous enemies along the way.

Perhaps one of these enemies could pop up in your story, causing trouble?

He, she or it could provide false information, or try to scare the detective away from solving the case.

Continued...

Whodunnit?

Who commited the crime?
How does your detective
work out the answer?
What happens when the
villain is caught?
Is the criminal banished to
another dimension?
Thrown in a supernatural
prison cell? Let off with a
warning? Handed over to
the human authorities?

The headless rider

Deep in the countryside, hushed tales are told of a headless rider, who gallops across the moors on horseback. One day, two friends are out on a hike, when they hear the sound of hooves getting louder...

Write your story title here.

Heads and tales

Stories about headless riders have existed for hundreds of years. They're told all over the world – from India and America, to Germany and Ireland.

In some stories, the headless rider is the ghost of a brave soldier who was beheaded in battle.

In others, the rider is the vengeful ghost of a highway robber.

Some tales tell the story of a hunter, whose head was lost in a hunting accident.

Write your own story about a headless rider. Who is this ghostly figure? What happened to its head?

Avoid specifics

Leaving gaps in your writing can unnerve your reader. When you only see glimpses of a ghost, your imagination fills in the rest.

Keep your descriptions vague and *unspecific*:

First the boy heard metal clinking. Straining his eyes, he could just make out the outline of a figure emerging from the mist. Was it... headless?

Rather than:

The boy looked up and saw a headless rider wearing a long black cloak and leather riding boots.

Live

Continued...

How does your story end?

What happens to the rider? Does it disappear back into the mist?

Is the rider trying to warn the two hikers about something? Perhaps there's a dangerous bend in the road ahead?

Some of the spookiest stories maintain a sense of mystery right until the very end.

Horror or hoax?

Some stories use spooky settings and events to trick readers into believing that they're reading a ghost story. But, in fact, the 'ghost' is fake and the real mystery is about the hoax: who is behind it, and why?

Write your story title here.

Write a story about a group of friends who investigate what *seems* to be a ghostly apparition. The beginning has been written for you.

Who are the friends investigating the 'ghost'? What's the connection between the apparition and the robberies?

Try coming up with a list of suspects and motives. Who might have a reason to create a fake ghost? Does someone want to scare the castle owner away? Steal things?

Here are some suggestions:

- The castle owner who's been arguing about money with several people in town.

- A greedy antiques dealer with a suspicious interest in the castle's silver collection.

- An arrogant millionaire who has tried, and failed, to buy the castle.

On the day the ghost appeared in town, other things started to *disappear*. At first it was just small items: keys went missing and flowers were taken from graves in the local cemetery. But, then, a precious silver goblet vanished from the castle on the hill, and everything changed...

74

Surprise them from behind

Throw your readers off the scent by encouraging them to believe they're reading a traditional ghost story.

- Keep the action in spooky places such as a gloomy old castle or an eerie cemetery.

- Use familiar ghostly descriptions, such as howling winds and bone-chilling cries.

- Drop red herrings to make the ghost seem real. Perhaps plants in the castle garden start to die or the earth around an old grave has been mysteriously disturbed?

Continued...

How to hoax?

Imagine how you might pretend to be a ghost. What would you need to pull off the hoax?

Add some of your own ideas to this list:

- White face-paint
- A smoke machine
- White sheets

Dead giveaway

While you're adding lots of ghostly details, drop clues that make your reader question what's really going on. Is the ghost real, or is it a human in disguise? For example:

Hiding behind a mossy gravestone, she noticed footprints in the mud. "What kind of ghost would leave these behind?" she wondered.

Continued...

Let's twist again

End with a bang by including a final plot twist in the last line of your story.

Perhaps there's more than one person behind the hoax? Or maybe the ghost turns out to be real after all?

As the police car drove away, no one noticed that real tears fell from the old stone statue...

Making a movie

Can you imagine any of the stories you've written in this book as a movie? Here's how to lay out a movie script.

A script is made up of a series of scenes. Each scene consists of action and dialogue.

For each new scene, write down whether it's going to be filmed inside (INT) or outside (EXT), and where and what time of day it is.

Describe what your characters look like the first time they appear.

SCENE ONE. EXT. FOREST - NIGHT

DANNY (11, scruffy, wearing a baseball cap) stands outside the front door of a falling-down cottage with his sister, LISA (13, tall, curly hair).

You can describe how a character speaks.

DANNY
I don't want to go in!
LISA
(whispering)
Scaredy cat! Scaredy cat!
DANNY
If you're so brave, why don't you go first?
LISA
Fine!

Lisa pushes open the door and runs through it.

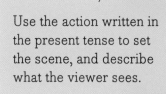

Use the action written in the present tense to set the scene, and describe what the viewer sees.

When you're writing dialogue, write the character's name in capitals, then write their speech underneath it.

Try writing the opening scene of one of your stories as a script.
(A scene is a part of a film that happens at a specific place and time.)

TITLE:

SCENE ONE.

Audition time!

Which actors would you choose to play your main characters? Imagining specific actors playing your characters can help bring them to life.

Location scout

Where could your story be filmed?

1.

2.

3.

Continued...

Soundtrack

Pick some music for your soundtrack, and list the track titles below.

1.

2.

3.

You could also include sound effects in your script, like these:

Groan Shriek YOWL Splatter

CRACK THWACK Gnaw SCRAPE

Squish   HISS   BANG   CRASH   Flutter
MOAN   ROAR   Psssssssst   Shuffle   Mutter

Story writing toolkit

Choosing a title

A good title grabs people's attention and makes them want to read the story. Titles should hint at what's to come, without giving too much away.

Here are some famous mystery and ghost story titles that might give you some ideas for your own.

This reveals the plot's main conflict (in this case, a murder).

You could keep the title clear and simple, like this.

Murder on the Orient Express

The Turn of the Screw

THE HOUND OF THE BASKERVILLES

Northanger Abbey

A Christmas Carol

THE YELLOW WALLPAPER

The Castle of Otranto

The Fall of the House of Usher

THE WOMAN IN WHITE

THE MYSTERIOUS AFFAIR AT STYLES

FRANKENSTEIN

The Adventure of the Speckled Band

This has a sense of intrigue – what's the hound, and who are the Baskervilles?

Add an element of surprise – Christmas stories aren't usually about ghosts, are they?

This focuses on the story's spooky setting.

You could try using a character's name.

Try creating your own titles, based on the story ideas below.

Story ideas:

Oliver's socks keep disappearing and he decides to find out why.

A fishing boat capsizes, and a mysterious ship comes to the rescue...

A family move into an old hotel and begin to renovate it. As they work, they realize it might be haunted.

Possible titles:

Everyday monsters

Even supernatural villains and master criminals can have very ordinary motives. Many of the best antagonists in mystery stories are exaggerated versions of average people with everyday feelings.

Try to imagine exaggerated versions of the characters below. Who are they, and what might they be capable of?

This example is what happens in
The Picture of Dorian Gray by Oscar Wilde.

Everyday character	Everyday reaction	Extreme version
A handsome man who loves his own good looks.	He takes constant photos of himself.	He wishes that a portrait of him would age, while he stays forever young... And his wish comes true.
A boy who worships a celebrity, and finds her knocking on his front door.		
A girl who's being bullied at school.		

Beginnings

Your story needs to be gripping from the very beginning.

Here are some ideas for beginnings – with tips to create your own on the right.

- Pramit spots a strange figure in one of his holiday photos. When he checks his pictures again, it seems to be in *all* of them.

- Julia arrives at school one morning, but no one can see her. She doesn't know why.

- The day after the Parker family move into a new house, they receive an anonymous letter warning them to get out.

Write your own gripping beginning to a story below.

Surprise start

You could begin your story with a shocking or surprising event, such as an accident, a natural disaster, or the appearance of a shrieking ghost.

Questions, questions

Try starting your story with a dramatic mystery that begs to be solved. For example, a character could wake up in a strange room, tied up, with no idea how he or she got there.

Flash forward

One way to grab your reader's attention is to begin at the most dramatic part of the story, and then go back in time to show how the character got to that point.

In the middle

You could think of the middle of your story as a rollercoaster, with lots of ups and downs. As soon as one problem is solved, introduce another, to keep the reader gripped, craving answers.

Add some more ups and downs to this ghost story plot.

A brother and sister decide to spend the night in a haunted house...

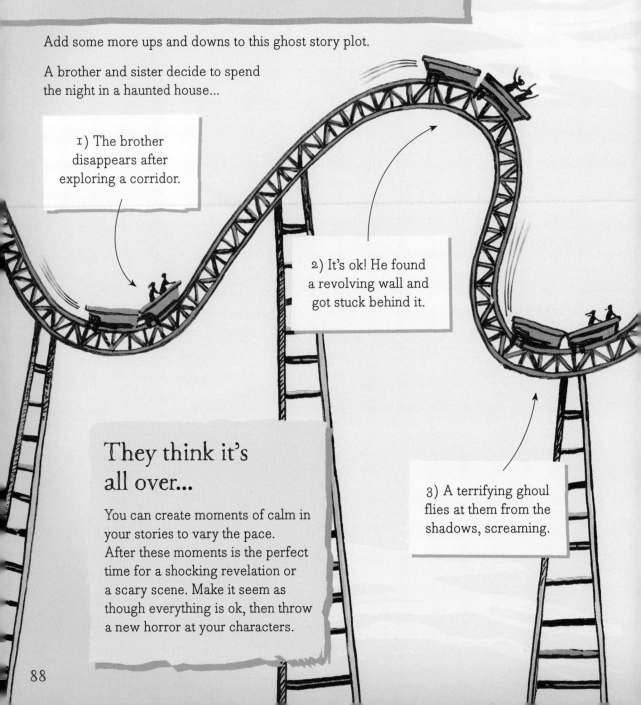

1) The brother disappears after exploring a corridor.

2) It's ok! He found a revolving wall and got stuck behind it.

3) A terrifying ghoul flies at them from the shadows, screaming.

They think it's all over...

You can create moments of calm in your stories to vary the pace. After these moments is the perfect time for a shocking revelation or a scary scene. Make it seem as though everything is ok, then throw a new horror at your characters.

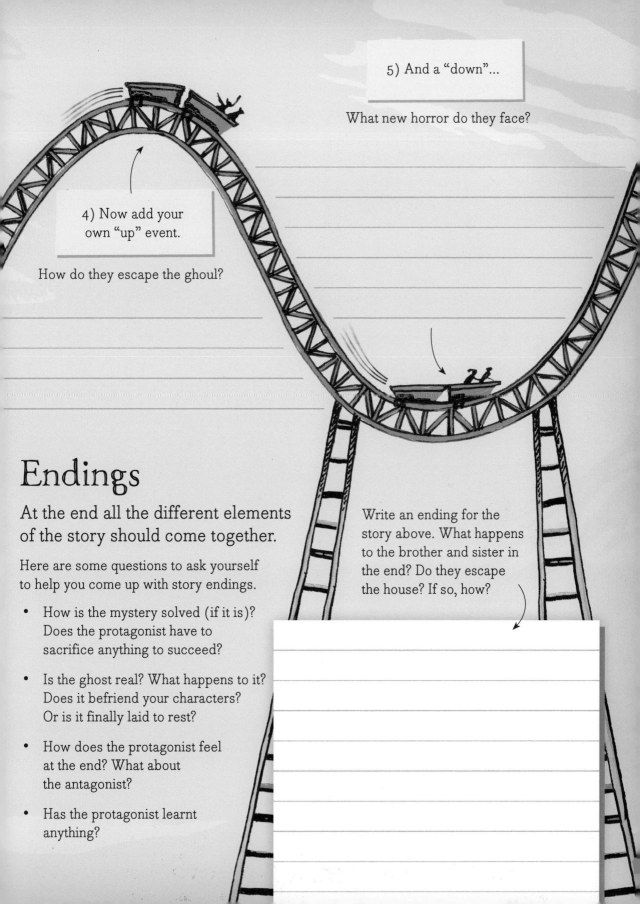

5) And a "down"...

What new horror do they face?

_____
_____
_____
_____
_____

4) Now add your own "up" event.

How do they escape the ghoul?

_____
_____
_____

Endings

At the end all the different elements of the story should come together.

Here are some questions to ask yourself to help you come up with story endings.

- How is the mystery solved (if it is)? Does the protagonist have to sacrifice anything to succeed?

- Is the ghost real? What happens to it? Does it befriend your characters? Or is it finally laid to rest?

- How does the protagonist feel at the end? What about the antagonist?

- Has the protagonist learnt anything?

Write an ending for the story above. What happens to the brother and sister in the end? Do they escape the house? If so, how?

Whose story?

The same basic plot could come out very differently depending on who is telling it.

First person (I or we)

This could be your main character, a sidekick, or even the antagonist. You're seeing the story through the eyes of one single character. For example...

> My new shoes for Granny's funeral had hardly any grip. I was terrified they'd start without me, so I started to run. That's when my foot slipped on the damp grass and I fell...

With the first person, the reader only ever knows what that character knows at any given point in the story. (The character doesn't know what he or she is falling into, for example.)

Second person (you)

This can pull your readers into the story, so they can experience the action as if it's happening to them.

> You lose your footing in the wet earth. Your arms flail helplessly against empty air and you are falling...

Third person (she, he or it)

Stories in the third person have a narrator who's outside the story, watching it. The narrator can know things the characters don't.

You could use a narrator who follows a single character, allowing you to see what he or she is thinking and feeling...

> "I can't be late for Granny's funeral," thought David as he rushed through the graveyard. Then he slipped on the damp grass and fell into a freshly-dug grave.

...Or try using a narrator who follows a number of characters and tells you about their thoughts and feelings.

> "I can't be late for Granny's funeral," thought David as he rushed through the graveyard. Then he slipped on the damp grass and fell into a freshly-dug grave.
>
> A figure watched from afar. "You'll regret that slip, child," she said.

Bring your setting to life

One way to create a vivid sense of place in your stories is to appeal to the five senses. What can your character hear? What does the air smell like?

Pick one of the settings below and describe a character arriving there, in the first person. Pay attention to his or her senses: sights, sounds, tastes, feelings or smells.

Settings

- An abandoned fairground at the edge of town.

- An old toy factory at midnight.

- A ruined castle where people say strange lights are sometimes seen at night.

- The house of an eccentric billionaire.

HUSKY COUGH

THE SCENT OF ROT

Smooth cold stone

CREAKING STAIRS

BAD BREATH

Dripping tap

ACRID STENCH

HAMMERING HEARTBEAT

Gun smoke

DAMP

Even more tips

Writing stories, like any skill, is something you get better at the more you do it.

Here are some tips to help you write your own mystery and ghost stories.

Vivid words

Try to use the most evocative words to describe what your characters are doing. Do they just 'walk' into the room? Or do they 'shuffle', 'edge' or 'dash'?

Instead of this...

> Pete looked up and saw a ghost. He was scared.

...try this alternative:

> Pete glanced up to see something ghostly flitting silently across the room. A wave of terror washed over him.

Pathetic fallacy

Create a heavy mood in your story with pathetic fallacy – a literary technique by which a character or narrator's emotions are reflected in nature.

Perhaps as your narrator feels tense, storm clouds gather outside? Or, when your narrator despairs, heavy rain starts to fall?

I don't believe it!

You could make your ghost story more plausible by including characters who don't believe that anything strange is going on until they're proved wrong. Here are some examples:

- A journalist is convinced that local stories about people going missing are just gossip, but then his brother disappears.

- A doctor who's spent her whole career dealing with scientific facts is forced to accept the supernatural after she encounters something strange in her attic.

Just add whirlwinds

Is your character angry, or is he or she a fierce whirlwind that's about to strike? Try to think of unusual images to describe your characters.

Help! I'm stuck

If you get stuck halfway through writing your story, try writing down three things that *definitely wouldn't* happen next. It could lead to unexpected ideas... Here's an example:

Henry buys a bottle of poison.

What *wouldn't* happen next:

1. He throws it away and decides to open a cake shop instead.

2. He thinks it's a bottle of shampoo and uses it to wash his hair.

3. He rubs the bottle and a genie comes out.

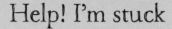

Of course you can trust me...

You could add another layer to your story by using a narrator who might not be telling the whole truth. Perhaps he or she has a habit of remembering things incorrectly, or perhaps there's a secret, which is only revealed at the end... Here are some examples:

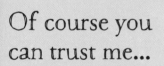

- A woman who is driven mad by a ghost.

- A boy who sets out to solve a kidnapping, but he's actually the kidnapper.

Avoid too many clichés

When you use an expression that's too familiar, this is called a cliché. If you find yourself using lots of familiar-sounding phrases, try rewriting some of them to make your story sound fresher.

Instead of this...

She let out a blood-curdling scream.

...try this:

Her scream was louder than a pack of howling hyenas.

Cut, cut, cut

If you've written long descriptions or rambling speeches that you find boring to read yourself, cut them.

Mystery and ghost words

CRYPTIC CLUE

TIP-OFF

Inkling

PREMONITION

Invisible

Deduce WITCHING HOUR

OVERHEAR BLACK MAGIC

STOMACH-CHURNING Vision

BANSHEE Menacingly

REVENANT MALEVOLENT PRESENCE

HALLUCINATION Undead

Knife edge Foreboding

Flickering candlelight DEMONIC

Ruined monastery SWOLLEN VEINS

Coated in dust IMPENETRABLE

Bribe RIGID

Cross-examine

CONSPIRACY

Sleuth

Enigmatic smile

Victim

BLACKMAIL

Mastermind

DODGY WITNESS

Cooperative

Occult

SILENT SCREAM

Garbled phone call

STORM THE BUILDING

Nest of spies

CATCH UNAWARE

Unravel

Yellow fog	Treat with suspicion	Caterwaul
Stench of death	BUG A PHONE	SLITHER
GLINTING LIGHT	Cover up	Talons
FRANTIC	FOUL PLAY	Twilight
Gnashed	Thwarted plan	Derelict
FROZEN MUSCLES	PLOY	HOODED
ICY FINGERS	SMELL A RAT	THRASHED
Pungent	Ouija board	Malicious
Muffled	EAVESDROPPER	Forbidding
SMUGGLE	Visitation	Quivered
Pounce	CREEPING DREAD	Hex
SHIFTING SHADOWS	Clinking chains	
SMEAR	Bulging	
HUNCH	Paranormal	
Vanished	Clanging bell	
TRANSLUCENT SKIN	CACKLE	
Following a lead	Echoed	

Acknowledgements

Story starters and tips written by
Megan Cullis, Matthew Oldham and Sarah Courtauld.

Illustrated by Pam Smy

Edited by Louie Stowell and Ruth Brocklehurst

Designed by Freya Harrison,
Laura Wood and Ian McNee

Usborne Quicklinks

For links to websites where you can find more tips and inspiration for writing terrifying ghost stories and thrilling mystery stories, go to www.usborne.com/quicklinks and type in the title of this book.
Please read our internet safety guidelines at the Usborne Quicklinks website.